Learniverse E World Ltd

Presents

Homo
The Adventure
of
Learning and Growing

© 2024 by Learniverse E World Ltd. All Rights Reserved.

No part of this book may be reproduced, distributed, or transmitted in any form or by any means, including photocopying, recording, or other electronic or mechanical methods, without the prior written permission of the author, except in the case of brief quotations embodied in critical reviews and certain other noncommercial uses permitted by copyright law.

All characters, events, and illustrations in this book are original creations by the author, based on real-life inspirations.

About the Author

"Preety, the visionary behind Learniverse E World Ltd, is an author and entrepreneur whose journey began on the serene shores of a small island. Her early experiences shaped a deep curiosity and an inmate understanding of the world around her. While traditional schooling offered structure, Preety found it limiting, her mind already exploring the boundless expanses of knowledge and discovery that lay beyond textbooks.

Her intellectual development flourished through a love of reading, writing and outdoor adventures, cultivating a lifelong passion for personal growth, education and critical thinking. Preety's early insights led her to appreciate the natural world and the value of factual, practical knowledge—key elements that now define her educational philosophy.

Preety's commitment to fostering intellectual growth is evident in her writing, which seamlessly blends educational content with engaging narrative that captivate young readers. With a global vision and a focus on long term impact, Preety is poised to make significant contributions to the world of education. Her goal is not only to engage young minds but to inspire a new generation of thinkers, leaders and innovators.

A Quote from the Author

"The Human brain is a universe unto itself, waiting to be explored. It's through the pursuit of knowledge and understanding that we can unlock its mysteries and shape better future "

Dedication

To the dreamers, the questioners and the explorers. This is for you. Learniverse E world Ltd built to inspire curiosity, ignite a love for learning and empower future leaders with essential skills. Whether through Homo's magical journey or through the lessons we teach, may you find the courage to seek knowledge, embrace new adventures and create a brighter tomorrow.

Acknowledgements

From the days of scribbling stories on the margins of notebooks to finally seeing my words come to life. I have always cherished a deep love for writing. Thought the opportunity to pursue this passion seemed distant for so long.

With heartfelt gratitude, I thank my partner for unwavering support and belief in this project. To my children, your admiration and joy inspire every word I write.

You are the foundation of my strength and creativity. This story is as much yours as it is mine. Thank you for being my foundation and my greatest source of strength.

Thank you for sharing your thoughts.
We appreciate your feedback.

Ky ★★★★★

An inspirational Journey!

Homo's adventure offers more than just excitement. It's a powerful lesson in overcoming challenges. The activities and reflective questions deepen the reader's connection, making it a story to revisit as life evolves. A perfect gift for any age, design to inspire for years to come.

Aleph ★★★★★

A must for schools and families!

Homo's story inspires creativity, curiosity, and perseverance. The engaging activities extend the story's impact, encouraging readers to think deep. Ideal for schools, family libraries or anyone. A great motivational and interactive read. Perfect for any occasion!

I draw ★★★★★

A story that lets your imagination soar!

The illustration is beautifully realistic but what truly stands out is how the story takes over as you read, allowing you to imagine your own scenes. While the images are wonderful, they become secondary to the vivid world your mind creates. A perfect blend of visuals and storytelling, sparking endless imagination. This is a smart creation.

Teacher ★★★★★

A Classroom Favourite!

As a teacher, Homo's Journey is perfect, it captivates my students and teaches valuable life lessons. The story sparks imagination, while the activities encourage critical thinking. My class loves it and can't wait for the next adventure! Highly recommended for any age classroom.

Contents

Chapter 1 Homo's Curiosity 1

Chapter 2 An Idea 3

Chapter 3 The Warning 6

Chapter 4 A Ray of Hope 11

Chapter 5 Ellie's Gentle Strength 13

Chapter 6 The Lazy Roar 17

Chapter 7 Homo's Big Discovery 19

"Reflect and Grow with Curiosity" 23

Activities 33

Homo

The Adventure of Learning and Growing

This book belongs to

....

Homo
The Adventure of Learning and Growing

Chapter 1
Homo's Curiosity

Once upon a time, in a distant land filled with wonder and mystery, there lived a curious being named Homo. But Homo wasn't just any being—he was very special, unlike any other animal in the vast green forest.

Homo
The Adventure of Learning and Growing

You see, Homo could think in ways that no other creature could. He could talk, dream, and ask big questions about the world around him. His mind sparkled with curiosity about everything around him, always buzzing with thoughts, and his eyes gleamed with the excitement of discovery.

The forest Homo lived in was a big green forest. It was lively and full of characters—playful monkeys swinging from trees, elephants bathing in the cool river, and birds serenading the treetops with their songs. Homo would often sit under the shade of the tallest tree and watch these creatures in awe.

He marvelled at the way they moved, communicated, and lived. But there was one thing that made Homo different from them, he had an itch for more, more knowledge, more adventures, and more answers to the endless questions bubbling in his mind.

Homo
The Adventure of Learning and Growing

Chapter 2
An Idea

One sunny morning, Homo had a grand idea—what if he could build something that no animal had ever built before? A shelter!

Homo
The Adventure of Learning and Growing

A place of his own. Using his clever mind, he gathered sticks and leaves, piecing them together into a cosy little shelter. It wasn't perfect, but to Homo, it was a masterpiece. Proud of his creation, Homo decided to throw a grand celebration, inviting all the animals of the forest for a feast.

As the tiger roared, its powerful call echoed through the forest, stirring the trees to life. Birds burst into song, their melodies dancing through the air. While, other animals joined in, creating a symphony of wild rhythms and harmonies. The jungle pulsed with energy, a celebration of sound as if the entire forest was singing in unison with the tiger's powerful roars.

They ate delicious fruits and nuts and danced until the sun went down.

Homo
The Adventure of Learning and Growing

Homo
The Adventure of Learning and Growing

Chapter 3
The Warning

But happiness, as Homo would soon learn, doesn't always last. Just a few weeks after the party, a fierce storm rolled through the forest. Homo had never felt fear like this before. Just a little while ago, everything had been perfect. The sun had warmed his skin, and the soft breeze made him feel like happiness would last forever.

But all of a sudden, the sky turned dark, like someone had pulled a giant, spooky blanket over the world. The wind began to gust fiercely and the trees that stood tall and strong were pulled out of the ground, flying through the air as if by some magic spell. Homo's cosy shelter, the one he had built with so much love, was torn apart, piece by piece, as the storm's wild hands ripped it apart like it was made of paper. The rain stung his skin, cold as ice, and the thunder rumbled so loudly it felt like the sky was yelling at him.

Homo's heart raced. The roar of the storm was deafening, drowning out his thoughts, filling his chest with a rising sense of dread. He could barely see through the sheets of rain, and every crash of thunder sent a jolt of terror through him. Desperately, he clung to a towering, mysterious stone slab, its surface cold and unyielding. Though he did not understand what it was, its immense presence offered a strange sense of protection, shielding his small shaking, trembling frame from the fury of the storm.

For the first time, *would this be the end?* he wondered.

It felt like the storm would never stop, like it would go on forever, and that no one would find him, alone in the storm's scary dance.

But then, deep inside him, something magical sparked. A tiny light, a flicker of hope, like a little star shining in the dark. Even though he was cold, wet, and afraid, Homo realised that

Homo
The Adventure of Learning and Growing

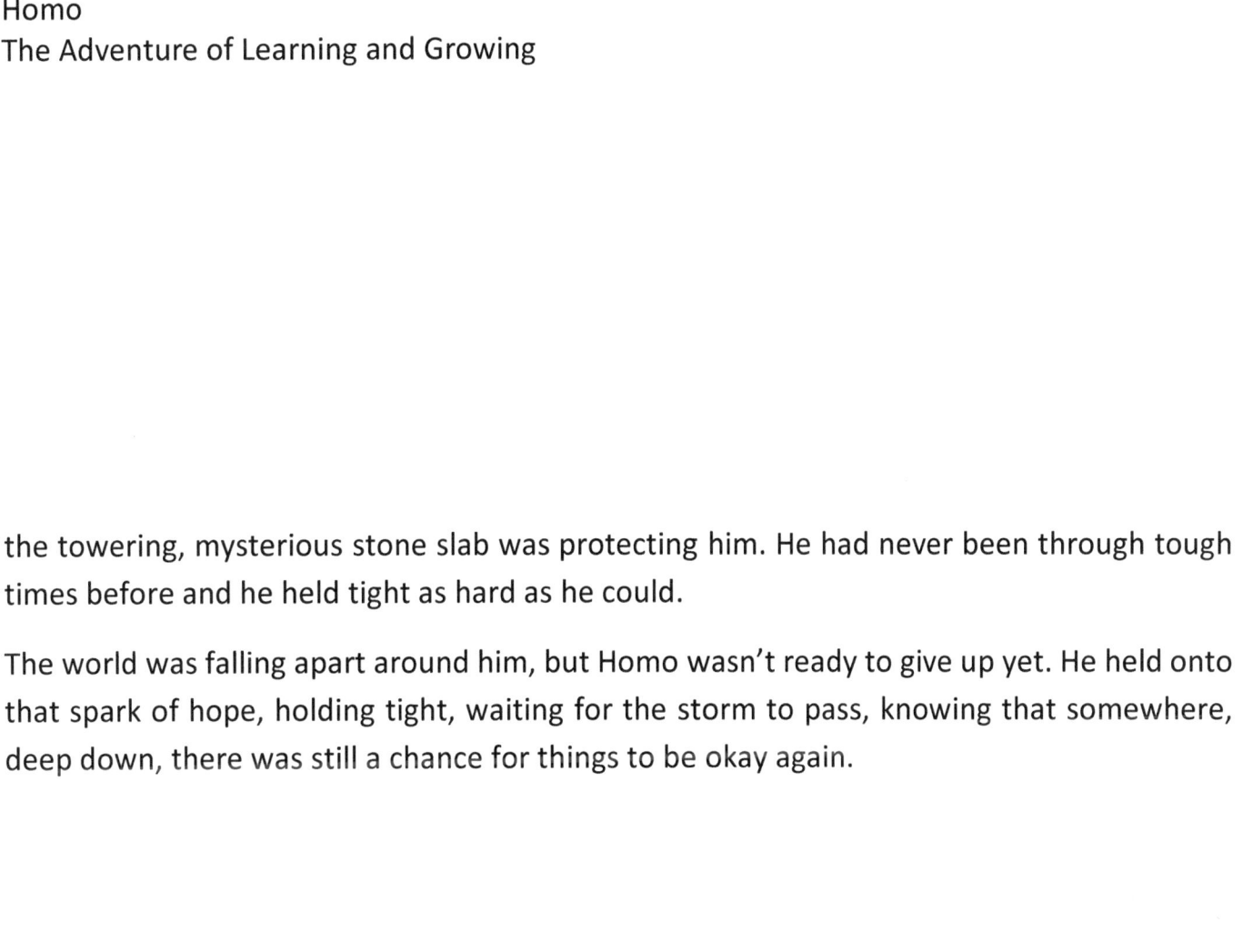

the towering, mysterious stone slab was protecting him. He had never been through tough times before and he held tight as hard as he could.

The world was falling apart around him, but Homo wasn't ready to give up yet. He held onto that spark of hope, holding tight, waiting for the storm to pass, knowing that somewhere, deep down, there was still a chance for things to be okay again.

Homo
The Adventure of Learning and Growing

Chapter 4
A Ray of Hope

When the storm finally passed, the world seemed to breathe again. The clouds parted, revealing the sun, whose rays danced on the wet forest floor. Homo carefully stepped out from behind the towering stone, feeling the warmth of the sun on his feet, and a surge of hope filled his heart. The storm had taken away his shelter, but it hadn't taken away his spirit. If anything, it made him stronger.

As Homo wandered through the forest, his feet stumbled upon something unexpected. His once-cosy shelter, the one he had worked so hard piecing together, had fallen apart! The sticks had turned mushy, the leaves were crumbling, and everything looked like it was melting back into the ground. Homo scratched his head and sighed. "What now?" he whispered, feeling a little sad and lost.

But Homo was no ordinary being—he never gave up that easily! He looked around the forest with his bright, curious eyes, and suddenly, an idea sparked. "There must be something stronger out here, something BIGGER!" And with that, his adventure began once again.

He wandered deeper into the forest. Along the way, Homo spotted an enormous, fallen tree trunk so large he could barely see the other end. "Whoa! That's what I need!" he reflected.

Homo
The Adventure of Learning and Growing

But how could he use something so gigantic? He stretched his arms, already feeling a little tired just thinking about it. "Hmm… maybe I could carve out a tunnel through the middle," he imagined, his eyes twinkling with excitement.

But first, he needed a break! Homo plopped down on a soft patch of moss, feeling his legs ache. As he rested, he heard the rush of the river nearby.

Peeking through the bushes, Homo gasped—the river was no longer the gentle stream he knew!

The storm had turned it into a wild, swirling flood. The water roared, sweeping away branches and rocks, but somehow, it was mesmerising. The water thundered as it cascaded down, a deep, resonant roar that filled the air. It surged with raw intensity, foaming and churning as it crashed against the riverbanks, its relentless power vibrating through the earth beneath. Homo watched the river with wide eyes, filled with wonder but also a creeping sense of worry. Just a while ago, he felt in control of his world, but now, for the first time, nature's wild force made him feel small. The river swirled and splashed, almost as if it had a mind of its own, and Homo couldn't shake the feeling that something unexpected was about to happen. "If the river could keep flowing, so could he!" thought Homo.

Chapter 5
Ellie's Gentle Strength

With renewed energy, Homo stood up. As Homo stared at the massive tree trunk, scratching his head in confusion, he had to admit—this was going to be tougher than he

Homo
The Adventure of Learning and Growing

thought. Just as he was about to give up and take another break, the ground beneath him shook with a gentle rumble. He turned around and saw his enormous friend, "Ellie the Elephant," strolling over with a grin on her face.

"Need a little help there, Homo?" Ellie exclaimed, her big ears flapping with excitement. "Oh, do I ever!" Homo laughed.

"This tree trunk is bigger than my whole shelter, and I need to move it up that hill!" He pointed to a higher spot where he could see the sun shining through the trees. "But... I can't do it alone."

Ellie smiled, her tusks gleaming in the sunlight. "As she imagined, she thought! I've got just the thing." With a mighty swoosh, she wrapped her strong trunk around the giant log and, with a grunt and a wiggle, lifted it off the ground!

"Whoa!" Homo's jaw dropped. "You make that look easy!"

But just as they started moving the trunk, something funny happened. A flock of little birds swooped down, chirping in excitement. "Look at that perfect new spot for a nest!" one of them squeaked. Without a delay, they started gathering twigs and fluff, making a cosy little nest right on top of the tree trunk as Ellie carried it!

Homo laughed. "I guess we're building a neighbourhood now!" As they climbed higher, Ellie carefully set the giant log down in its new place.

Huffing and puffing, Homo finally got the giant trunk where he wanted it. He looked at it with pride. "This will be my new place!" He imagined himself climbing through the tunnel, decorating it with leaves, making secret rooms inside! Even though he was tired, he felt that spark of excitement again.

The birds fluttered around, adding final touches to their nests, chirping joyfully. Everything seemed to be coming together.

Homo
The Adventure of Learning and Growing

Chapter 6
The Lazy Roar

Unexpectedly, a deep roar echoed through the trees. Homo turned and saw—of all animals—the tigers lounging nearby, watching the whole thing with their lazy eyes.

One tiger let out a long, lazy yawn, its mouth stretching wide before closing with a soft sigh, its eyes half-lidded in contentment as it curled up. "Nice work, Ellie... Homo... we'll just sit here and make sure you are protected." The other tigers stretched, their claws digging into the ground, but didn't move an inch.

Homo couldn't help but giggle. "Typical tigers! They always have the loudest roar but the smallest effort. Ellie rolled her eyes playfully. "Some animals, huh?"

But as funny as it all was, Homo knew there was something more to think about. As they continued their work, Homo began to ponder.

"Why do the tigers just sit and roar while we do all the work?" he wondered out loud. And then it hit him. Not everyone helps in the same way! Some might make noise, others might build nests, and some—like Ellie—are always ready to lend a hand (or trunk!)

Homo nodded, realising the truth in Ellie's signs. "I guess you're right. Everyone has their own way of contributing, even if it's not always obvious."

Homo
The Adventure of Learning and Growing

Chapter 7
Homo's Big Discovery

Homo realised something important. In life, it's not about who's the loudest or the strongest. It's about who takes action and thinks of others. Homo thought for a moment, feeling a sense of pride. "Maybe the tigers are simply different. But that doesn't mean I stop trying to help my friends."

As the sun dipped lower and painted the sky with pinks and oranges, Homo stood next to Ellie, the giant log now in an attempt to create a new shelter for Homo and the birds. He smiled, knowing that with a bit of teamwork and clever thinking, anything was possible. Yes! "I can do this!" he thought. Feeling the warmth of hope bubble inside him.

And who knows—maybe one day, the tigers would help too. But for now, Homo and his friends had all they needed: cosy new shelters, a bit of fun, and the joy of working together.

The forest had given him the tools, and his imagination would do the rest. With that, Homo knew his adventure was just beginning.

Again, Homo invited his friends to celebrate his achievement. But this time, the party wasn't just about fun. It was a testament to Homo's resilience, his ability to learn, adapt, and grow. As the animals danced and laughed, Homo felt a deep sense of peace. He realised that the

Homo
The Adventure of Learning and Growing

storm, while terrifying, had taught him something important: challenges could be overcome with courage, creativity and hope.

Days turned into weeks, weeks into months, and Homo continued his journey of exploration. He learned how to craft tools from stones, how to plant seeds to grow food, and how to build stronger shelters. Homo's thirst for knowledge never faded. Along with his forest friends, he built not just shelters but entire villages. They shared their discoveries and inventions, and together, they thrived.

But who was Homo? Was he just a curious being from a faraway forest? Or was he something more? As time passed, Homo and his friends spread across the land. They built great cities, created art, invented languages, and shaped the world in ways no one could have imagined. Homo had a secret, you see—he was the beginning of something extraordinary and his story, a story of wonder, courage, and endless curiosity, is still being written today.

Homo
The Adventure of Learning and Growing

Homo
The Adventure of Learning and Growing

Homo
The Adventure of Learning and Growing

"Reflect and Grow with Curiosity"

1) What do you think made Homo different from the other animals in the forest? How do you think his curiosity helped him build his shelter?

A. Homo was the fastest animal, which helped him gather materials quickly.

B. Homo could talk to animals, which made them help him build his shelter.

C. Homo had a special ability to think and ask questions, which helped him figure out how to build his shelter.

D. Homo could sing beautifully, which attracted the best building materials.

Correct Answer:

2) Why do you think Homo invited all the animals to his party? What do you think he wanted to share with them?

A. He wanted to show off his new house and celebrate with his friends.

B. He wanted to ask them for more building supplies.

C. He wanted to make them jealous of his house.

D. He wanted to practise his singing skills.

Correct Answer:

Homo
The Adventure of Learning and Growing

3) When the storm destroyed Homo's house, how do you think he felt? What made him decide to rebuild his house even stronger?

A. He felt happy and wanted a change, so he rebuilt his house stronger.

B. He felt sad and scared but wanted to prove he could overcome the challenge.

C. He felt indifferent and decided to move to a new forest.

D. He felt annoyed and wanted to take revenge on the storm.

Correct Answer:

4) Homo learned to use new materials to make his house better. How do you think learning and adapting helped him overcome the challenges he faced?

A. It allowed him to build a more beautiful house, even though it wasn't stronger.

B. It helped him create a house that could withstand future storms.

C. It made his house look different but didn't help with the storm.

D. It made him popular with the other animals, who helped him build.

Correct Answer:

Homo
The Adventure of Learning and Growing

5) Why do you think the storm was an important part of Homo's story? What did he learn from it that helped him in the future?

A. The storm taught him how to dance in the rain.

B. The storm showed him how to build a house that looks good.

C. The storm was a challenge that taught him to rebuild better and be resilient.

D. The storm made him realise he should move to a different forest.

Correct Answer:

6) Homo and his friends-built villages and cities after learning new things. How do you think their discoveries changed their world? What can we learn from their achievements?

A. Their discoveries made the forest more crowded and noisier.

B. Their discoveries led to building new homes and improving their lives.

C. Their discoveries made them forget about the old ways of living.

D. Their discoveries led them to leave the forest and explore the ocean.

Correct Answer:

Homo
The Adventure of Learning and Growing

7) In the story, Homo's journey involves exploring and learning. Why do you think it's important to be curious and to ask questions about the world around us?

A. Being curious helps us make friends and win games.

B. Curiosity helps us learn new things and solve problems, leading to better solutions.

C. Curiosity makes us less interested in what we already know.

D. Curiosity is only important if we want to become famous.

Correct Answer:

8) What qualities did Homo show that helped him succeed? How can we show these same qualities in our own lives?

A. He showed laziness and only worked when he felt like it.

B. He showed determination and creativity, which helped him overcome obstacles.

C. He showed anger and blamed others for his problems.

D. He showed shyness and avoided challenges.

Correct Answer:

9) **Based on the story, what kind of being do you think Homo might be? What clues in the story led you to this idea?**

A. Homo is a bird because he loves to sing.

B. Homo is a monkey because he climbs trees.

C. Homo is a special being that can think, talk, and build things.

D. Homo is an elephant because he can swim in rivers.

Correct Answer:

10) **What do you think Homo's story teaches us about handling challenges and learning new things?**

A. It teaches us to avoid challenges and stick to what we know.

B. It teaches us to face challenges with courage, learn from them, and grow stronger.

C. It teaches us to ignore problems and hope they go away.

D. It teaches us to compete with others to show we are better.

Correct Answer:

Homo
The Adventure of Learning and Growing

"Reflect and Grow with Curiosity"

CORRECT ANSWERS

C, A, B, B, C, B, B, B, C, B

A Rhyme for Homo

"Homo's Heart"

In a world so vast, with skies so wide,
lived a soul named Homo, full of pride.
He wandered far, both near and high,
With dreams as bright as the morning sky.

Through storms and winds, through rain and sun,
He learned that life's a race never done.
Each step he took, both bold and slow,
taught him lessons he'd come to know.

Not all will help, not all will care,
but in his heart, there's love to share.
With Ellie's strength, the gentle guide,
He learned that help comes side by side.

Homo
The Adventure of Learning and Growing

Yet tigers LOUD roared, but did not HELP,
for lazy hearts dim their light.
Homo saw through all the noise,
that true strength comes in humble poise.

He built his dreams with hands and heart,
for every end is just a start.
Through every challenge, every bend,
He found that hope does never end.

So, children, listen, be like him,
When the road is tough and chances slim,
with courage bright and love so true,
there's nothing that you cannot do.

Homo
The Adventure of Learning and Growing

Activities

Here are a few activities to engage with the story of Homo.

1. Try and write your rhyme.

2. Draw your vision of Homo.

3. Design Homo's Future Shelter.

Homo
The Adventure of Learning and Growing

Activity Page

Homo
The Adventure of Learning and Growing

Activity Page

Homo
The Adventure of Learning and Growing

Activity Page

Homo
The Adventure of Learning and Growing

Activity Page

Homo
The Adventure of Learning and Growing

Activity Page

Months after, Homo and his friends continued to work on their shelters. The tigers, however, seemed to grow bolder. One night, they heard a strange, echoing sound coming from deep within the forest. Curiosity piqued, Homo decided to investigate. He gathered a small group of his bravest friends and ventured in the unknown.

As they delved deeper into the forest, the noise grew louder and more mysterious. Suddenly, a blinding light erupted from the trees, illuminating a hidden cave. Intrigued and a little scared, Homo and his friends cautiously approached the entrance.

Homo
The Adventure of Learning and Growing

The cave was dark and filled with an eerie silence. As they ventured deeper, they heard a faint whisper, as if someone was calling out to them. Gathering their courage, Homo and his friends stepped into the unknown, their fate hanging in the balance.

What awaited them inside was a mystery that would change their lives forever.

Activity Page

Homo
The Adventure of Learning and Growing

End of Book One

www.ingramcontent.com/pod-product-compliance
Lightning Source LLC
Chambersburg PA
CBHW050739110526
44590CB00002B/31